Listening for Water

8/9/U
To Alexander
Jacadze
+ Susan - from Naomi Chase
for your
concern + the
pleasure + the
sorrow my
care

*L*istening for Water, a first collection of poems by Naomi Feigelson Chase, celebrates the epiphanies of life with vivid, moving detail. This new edition is designed and illustrated by John Murray.

*L*istening for Water was originally published by the Archival Press, Cambridge, MA in 1980.

N aomi Feigelson Chase is also the author of *The Underground Revolution: Hippies, Yippies and Others* and *A Child Is Being Beaten.*

S ome of these poems have appeared in:

Dark Horse for "At the Beach," 1977 and "Movie," 1978

Poets On for "Fire Island," 1979 and "Icons," 1980

Radcliffe Quarterly for "The Good Brown Housewife," 1979

The Real Paper for "*Homo Protectus*," and "My Father Dreams His Life, My Father Dreams His Father," 1978

Terra Poetics for "My Mother Sent Me Gifts" and "Winter Landscape," 1980

Triton College, Passages VI for "Wiracocha," 1980

Yankee for "Letter from a Recluse," 1981

Xanadu for "Floating," 1980

For Elizabeth and Jonathan

Listening For Water

ISBN   0-915822-05-9 (Paperbound)
ISBN   0-915822-06-7 (Microfiche)

Library of Congress Cataloging in Publication Data
Chase, Naomi Feigelson 1932
Listening for Water: poetry.
Library of Congress 80-800 70

Signed copies of this edition of *Listening for Water* are available through Buckley-Little Book Catalogue Company, Inc., Route 100, Millwood, New York 10546, from the author, or from selected bookdealers.

C over Design and Illustrations by John Murray.

John Murray is a painter and graphic artist whose work has been widely exhibited. He has been a Finalist and a Fellow of the Massachusetts Artists Foundation and in 1986 received the L.E. Sissman Award for excellence in the arts.

Layout by Paul Coyle

Contents

Listening for Water

Naomi Feigelson Chase

Floating

I

Restless all night,
at dawn he dreams
the empty beach,
stretched pale against the washing of the sea.
The sun bursts up.
He sets his towel beside his shoes.
Then, in his old white bathing cap,
floating on his back, he squints
at the Italian painting of a sky.
In a picture he once saw,
an apple floats above a sharp-faced man
who longs to eat it.

II

At the table with his dinner,
with his daughters,
he says nothing, wants nothing.
Bending over him, his nurse cuts his meat.

Doors slam, his grandchildren
rush in from the beach.
He frowns and the wind drops in their faces.
They sit and eat.

III

At night, he does not sleep.
He balances his checkbook,
dictates letters he will never send,
and tells the nurse to throw away his belt, his socks.

Months ago he withdrew from his face,
from his body, slumped in a rented, rolling chair,
from his foot strapped to plastic.
Sometimes he strokes the fingers
of his useless arm.

My Mother Sent Me Gifts

My mother sent me gifts in metal laundry boxes
when I went to college. Tucked among the clean clothes,
Rye-Krisp, pale green sickle pears.

My mother shopped on sale,
three dozen peach towels still in cartons.
She sent nightgowns when I married,
though she knew I never wore them.
She sent gloves. The color came off
on my hands, blue, red.

My mother spoke in Hebrew, English, Yiddish,
sad in all tongues.
She wrote to me daily, starting with the weather,
anger, always ended love.

Every week she had her nails lacquered
rose or crimson red. At home she wore
a printed cotton,
black, laced shoes, white socks.

I found brocade kimonos when she died,
satin nightslips, new, in tissue.
What was she saving her life for
as she sat in her housedress, hands in her lap,
long white fingers, long red nails, white half-moons?

At the Beach

I

The children play Monopoly all day,
moving the game from room to room,
while outside, rain drips steadily
on the left-hand wash of the sea.

II

Everyone wears a G-string at the beach.
Bearded men with hair to their shoulders,
girls with mirrors in their minds.

At Enid's party,
Gretta came in drag.
Odessa, dark and buxom,
lay face up on the floor,
to see if the lady
in the buttocks-length dress
was naked underneath.
"Here," said the woman
in the see-through jumpsuit,
"I have nothing to hide."
The men go after her with flashlights,
but it's all a put-on
over flesh-colored tights.
Looking for something real,
Herb walks into the kitchen
to fondle the potatoes.

III

The sculpture garden next door
wheels and whirls.
"Junk on junk,
it's all balance,"
Leonard explains.
Nothing is stuck together,
and if the wind blows it down at night,
he builds it over
the next day.

Fire Island

This sand bar called the Island
shifts daily.
That house on the blowing dunes
with the yellow window frames
might be floating out to sea tomorrow.

Everything moves here,
sea shells,
reed grass,
fences.
The sand drifts blur all boundaries.
The dune fence sags into the bay.

Nothing holds,
but the shells I fix,
glued lip to lip around my mirror,
framing my summer face.

Homo Protectus
to Leonard Bocour

An arm here,
a leg there,
Leonard's sculpture garden
makes a path
from his house
to the sea.

The dump is his quarry.
With a broken umbrella,
a porcelain sink,
a bicycle wheel,
he makes a man.

Wheel whirls,
sink and umbrella
hang precisely.
Leonard names it
Homo Protectus.
It lasts all day,
fragile as love,
made of old parts
in perfect balance.

Stories

To Elizabeth

I

Together we packed the car
to accommodate your heap of goods,
and now it's taking us to your new life.
The Saratoga trunk I gave you
with its lid of hammered flowers
hunches on the back seat,
a portion of your life, moving
out of mine.

Speeding down the turnpike,
we talk, talk,
weaving again the endless silk
between us.

When you first walked,
you pulled yourself up,
your fist on the glass table, laughing.

At your dorm, unpacking,
I cannot bear to leave you, but I do,
returning to an empty car.

Then, driving home, a traffic jam for miles
stalls thought. It's hard to concentrate
in second, first, second, always shifting.
Finally, I'm moving, time to review
years I spent preparing you to go,
while I, like a novice, was
unprepared for this silence.

II

Our marriage was spare
as our apartment,
white rooms,
waiting for love to warm the walls.

My old piano needed tuning,
but our washer, dryer,
and refrigerator
were new and worked.

We must eat and soil,
robes must be laundered,
only the thin silk that wraps the heart
keeps itself immaculate;
only the pump that spins the blood,
warming the toes on bare sheets,
flushing the fingers on bare shoulders,
knows its own cycle.
A handful of quarters will not start it up.

River, park, drive, all life moved
outside our windows.
I thought we'd stay there until we died,
not knowing how soon that was.

III

Mother, you had nothing to teach but anger, and
I read it like a text nailed to the door.

I can hear you speaking Hebrew
with your father, laughing,
but you and I never talked.

I remember sitting backwards on the covered toilet
while you braided my hair.

You called everyone "stupid."
"I don't drink," you said.
"I don't play cards."

Bitter plaque filled your veins,
like sludge, silting up a river.

Now I will never hear your story
and you will never hear mine.

Last time I saw you in the nursing home
in a pink robe,
tied to the chair,
the fork shaking in your hand,
you asked who I was.

I remember you lacing your corset.
It had stays and hooked tight under your breasts.
You disappeared into it, pulling and tying.

Birthday Poem
to Jonathan

I

I knew you before your birth,
carried your shadow like undeveloped film,
needing only a dark room, time,
the proper bath.

I wanted a blue-eyed boy,
pictured you at the beach,
laughing, holding my hand as we walked.
I never thought of you grown.

II

In your muscled belly,
how can you imagine one
who is you and not you?

While you were moving inside me,
I spun the connecting threads.

The night you were born, I ate too much,
not expecting your company so soon.
Then I worried,
waiting for the water to break,
waiting for the labor to start.

At your birth,
the pain travelled up to my mouth, and
we screamed together with the shock of air.
Then, still puffed up but hollow,
I was sewn up like a ripped bag,
and you moved on to your next home.

Winter Landscape

Like rain without a landscape,
lines about my father
fall through my dreams.

I see him crumpled among pillows
in a hospital crib,
tears like raisins
in his gingerbread face.

Years when I came home from school,
arriving late in the December station,
he greeted me on the empty platform,
brisk and fur-collared.

Last night I dreamed I was wearing black.
There were crowds and flowers.
"It's not my wedding," I said,
"It's not my wedding."

Now the train pulls
across the winter nightscape,
outside, the trees, a silvery mass,
each needle framed in ice.

My Father Dreams His Life,
My Father Dreams His Father

In a storm of white-armed trees,
my father dreams his life,
he waltzes down the Ringstrasse.
Soft evening promenades beneath the leaves.

My father dreams his father,
the comfortable merchant
who sells on installment.
Sunday he rides out in his *einspanner* to collect.

At home, his mother in full-sleeved lace,
frowns under piled-up hair.
The *madchen für alles*
stands on the table to light the lamp.

My father dreams his father
still tall in his coffin,
burned out by a fire in his body,
the blonde mustache singed black.

In America, wiping the German from his tongue,
my father translates himself into a lawyer,
defends Communists with Darrow,
leads hunger marches.

In Congress, he wears a cape like FDR.
As Judge, he never takes a gift
over three dollars.

My father reads the newspapers at table
while my mother maligns his relatives.
He measures his cholesterol
like a spiritual temperature.

After dinner, he journeys over figured carpets
bargained home from Istanbul,
fingers his ivory ladies, and blushes
at the bronze goddess of Angkor Wat.

My father dreams of wheelbarrows
heaped with paper marks
careening down the Ringstrasse,
crashing over gentlemen in cloaks.
Their black boots pursue him over the ocean.

My father dreams himself the Judge in the mirror,
growing and shrinking in his robes,
dreams the bare-armed beauty in her silver frame,
now thinning and nodding
downstairs in her geriatric crib.

"Is this all," asks the Judge in the mirror,
"A yellowing pile in the newspaper morgue,
a footnote in the Congressional Record?"

The gentleman in robes steps out of the mirror.
"Come, *Landsman*," he whispers,
"We will go back to the old country together."

Finding the Self

Humming down Broadway,
I want to fling out my arms and spin like a top,
twirl like a Sufi, blurring to a frenzy,
my robe a dark sail filled with wind.

I want to paint my face with prayer
and drink peyote with the Huichol,
capture the sacred cactus,
shaking my feathered wand.

Grunting and thrusting,
like a Master of Kung Fu,
I would initiate the timid self
into hard-bellied mysteries.

I want to fall into the vacuum,
floating free,
at 86th and Broadway.

After-Image

At the top of Mt. Desert
I held the camera near the ground
and snapped the gray Maine rock we'd climbed.

Now I scan blow-ups for shadows of myself,
wondering at daisies hidden in brown tufts
and life-green patches I never noted.

By the pond, I caught Gordon
in a widening road of birches,

Elizabeth, walking on rocks,
arms clasped behind her, like a young Darwin
searching for fish in iridescent waters,

and in the woods, a spider,
among trailing roots and vines.
Shining now, like a Kirlian gleam,
it startles, X-ray white in its white web.

My grandfather, soon to be blind, stands,
eyes dark to the sun glinting on his glasses.

The children, infants in my arms,
grow up.

At Cuzco, I snapped an Indian mother weaving,
with her baby on her back.
Now I see a black dog prowls
at the edge of the picture,
and in the foreground, a two-year old,
hand out, begs as her mother taught her.

I am there as the composing eye,
fixing, but unfixed.
I sift the photographs for clues,
stirring the shaded water.
At the root of the tree,
I am caught in the spider's web.
In that phosphorous net, someday,
I'll find my bones.

Movie

The sun was so bright, the air
so clear, so blue. The dog
looked so pleased with himself,
crossing. The road, as it hit him,
like a bright, endless movie,
reels on in my mind, blue sky,
clear bright day, a dog,
repeating itself, dying.

Icons

Wrapped in my sister's letter,
three color polaroids,
snapshots of my mother,
taken in the nursing home.

A voice below my voice cried *Mama!*
Not that blue-robed relic
before a printed curtain,
looking monkey curious,
papered to her bones.

What is it we preserve in you
as we tend the mother-thought
that fleshed us,
keeping you washed and powdered,
taking birthday pictures,
propping your life before your dinner tray?

You are lost in your own shadow,
your pureed treats,
your honeyed juices,
read like auguries for chloride and creatinine.

What remains of you is catabolic matter—
you're breaking down, the doctor says,
the nurse says you are heavier—
your muscles stiffening,
your body obdurate as stone.

Mother, when you die,
I'll wash you with a muslin cloth,
and wrap you like the Incas wrapped their Kings
in gold cocoons forever,
to rest sacred and unborn.

Letter from A Recluse*

I deny that I am a recluse.
Neither am I an unsociable hog.
It's true visitors are inconvenient.
I wrote that to spare you as well as me.

Since you must know,
I never had a bed in my house.
I do my own work.
No man or woman lives nearby.
The railroad skirts me by four miles
and few letters are delivered here.
I fish, paint.
It's the only life
permits me to mind my own business.

I'd like to do that lithograph
for your catalogue,
"But what's the hurry," said the King of Prussia.
When I get ready
I will send for a stone.

*Adapted from the letters of Winslow Homer to Louis Prang.

Wiracocha, the Jaguar

I

There in the dark
jaguars walk the streets of Lima,
lifting delicately their great blond paws,
slipping through the shadows,
past the shoeboys sleeping
crouched at the curb,
where white-gloved footmen spin the golden doors,
at the Grand Hotel Bolivar.

II

Far from Mira Flores, a stench rises,
the heavy musk of pigs, children,
dung burning.
A million huts stagger up sand mountains,
where tourist buses shuttle
from Lima to Pachacamac.

III

The jaguars do not go to Pachacamac,
only German Ursula with wattled arms,
leading a phalanx of tourists.
She barks into her bullhorn
and conjures up an ancient shrine
from a hill of rubble.

Out in the distance,
while jaguars watch with glowing eyes,
the Inca kings sit wrapped in gold
in their sacred niches,
stare as their Father, flaming,
slips through his necklace of clouds
into the sea.

IV

Wiracocha, the jaguar-creator was there,
when the sun fled from its garden
where gold llamas grazed, gold shepherds herding,
when the gold plumes came nodding down,
the great round coins, a honeyed stream
melting into Spanish ships.

V

There in the dark,
like Ataphualpha's ransom, their fur gleaming,
the jaguars slip down Union Street,
past the peddlers on their plastic squares,
the steaming maize, the spiced fish,
past the brown-toothed Indian.

At the Plaza des Armas,
eyes shining,
they pass the guards drowsing under gold helmets,
mount the steps of the Cathedral,
dropping hot mounds of dung,
pissing steam fountains.
They move to the vault where Pizarro lies
in a glass casket,
his yellowed bones a dried locust.
In the heat of their eyes,
the glass shatters,
the bones tremble.

Innocence on Ermine

In the picture before me, Innocence sits on ermine.
She shows a milk-white shoulder;
her skirt, looped up, displays a thigh.
She slips a wreath of flowers
around a ram's neck. He frowns.

An old house, a flickering fire.
Two hundred years ago,
a woman drew fresh baked loaves
from a sooty beehive oven.
At night did she imagine me
as I sit listening for ghosts?

In my daughter's room upstairs,
in the African basket of single socks,
the cat sleeps in a warm circle,
like my daughter when she rested in my belly.
Now she sleeps elsewhere, curled with her lover.

And far away, my son dreams himself a hero,
Hercules running,
his shoulders padded with vanity,
his head helmeted in plastic.

Vegetable Love

The eggplant hides shyly
its drooping purple globes,
shiny, discrete,
among the dense, stiff leaves.

The virginal tomato shocks easily,
is best started under glass.
When green and hard,
old, ornamental love-apple, it
blushes, and softens red.

The squash lies among the eggplant,
heavy and narrow-waisted,
dreaming how it sprouted
from the blossom's throat,

Showy, yellow, velvet
head dangling on its spindly stalk,
the fragile nasturtium climbs the tomatoes.
The marigold, blunt and brilliant,
traps the beetle in its orange heart,

while the small, exuberant parsley
stretches its curly fronds in all directions,
hides nothing, digs its roots in,
and like the ancient, self-sufficient fern,
prepares to winter over.

The Good Brown Housewife

Now that there is no one to remind
to wash their hands,
she washes her own,
leaving the garden dirt
in clots
under her nails,

thinking how much foolish time
she's spent with brooms,
sweeping out the earth
she'll lie in.

In the Waiting Room

Poster Amazons on horseback
ride the walls.
A woman screams,
painted behind five black bars.

My daughter sits barefoot
like a country girl.
Curls fall down her cheeks.
Her fist hides her mouth
like the thumb she sucked
in her crib,
warm bundle,
knees out,
sole to sole.

When Brunhild,
the traffic coordinator,
in black beret and bulging breasts
comes to the door,
my daughter will descend
to the underworld,
pull down her pants,
put up her legs,
while the doctor,
like a careful housewife,
vacuums the waste out.

Robbed

He razored the screen,
kicked in the glass, and
stepped through the bathroom window.

I'm sure the dog greeted him,
followed him from room to room,
dusting his pants with her tail.

In the kitchen, he hung my binoculars
around his neck,
fed the dog a biscuit,
grabbed a cold ham
to eat when he was through.

Speakers gaped
where he ripped off covers.
He kicked through drawers,
kicked shoes along the closet floor,
as though booting through leaves.

My grandmother's silver buckles
bulged in his pockets.
He jammed my mother's lapis earrings into
dirty trousers.
He took my daughter's baby pearls.

At night I hear him when
a radiator chokes,
when a branch slaps the house.
His face turned from the moon,
he steps up the trellis,
crushing flowers,
climbs through my locked dreams, and
night after night,
cuts the screen...

Music Mother

I am twelve years old, my hair in braids,
my pedal feet in Oxfords.
I practice my scales, stepping up ivory.
Only the music, the metronome's heart-beat,
and my teacher's voice are real, as I sit at the piano,
playing Mozart, in Pittsburgh, Pennsylvania.

I love Mrs. Karenyi, my piano teacher.
My mother calls her a "blue-stocking," but she wears
ordinary nylons on her bony knees.
Great paintings cut from magazines
fill her staircase wall.
They are even in the bathroom.

Alone as I practice, I think of her, alone,
in her crisp, gray skirt and silky blouse.
She sits by a brass bed with a white cover, lilacs
in a vase by the table. She reads.

Sometimes she invites me to dinner,
chicken paprikash and dumplings her mother
made in Hungary, so perfect in silver bowls
at first I am afraid to eat.
Then she opens her phonograph, takes out a record,
tells me the great Landowska, just for me,
will now play Mozart on the clavichord.

Years later, when I learn she is dead,
I buy a wooden metronome,
and sit by the piano.
I see her in the room where she died,
smell the lilacs, the paprikash.
I am there as her Landowska,
my hair in a bun, a rose on my black dress.
My feet on the pedals,
I bow my head and play.
Just for her,
this Mozart.

Longer than the Hundred Years' War

Bitter as the War of the Roses,
longer than the Hundred Years' War,
we fought in single combat,
in and out of love.
We overturned tables,
left blood on telephone wires.

In our cell,
bound at the wrist by hoops of steel,
we plotted treason against our lives.

At court masques, I saw your wife,
robed in your name, your fur cloak.
My coffee cup spattered
your cream-colored office walls.

Mouths hot, we spat each other out
in last battles.
Horses rearing, we backed off,
lunged and fell, tangled in arms.

A hundred years have passed and no one is King.
I have wiped your name from the tombstone.
We are buried elsewhere.

Flowering Plum

The flowering plum outside our window
feels its roots beneath the house.
Last year's hurricane slashed the trunk,
but could not reach them.

Under the old quilt with its frayed connections—
seams that many fingers smoothed,
brown and red squares that many hands set out—
we lie swaddled in self-regard.

You want quilt, matches, me,
all on your side.
Sometimes I want talk between us.
Sometimes I want a wall.

Eight years we've spun in our own seasons
like the moon. It turns from us tonight,
lights other windows. In the dark,
our ivory faces pulse with a cold light.
And still it's spring outside.

The garden calendar says,
"Plant peas, if the ground is not too wet."

For a time, veins shrank,
sapwood listened for water,
the tree waned.
Now it blooms, a cloud of pale white faces.